AF604427

First Knowledges for younger readers

Caring for Country

Bruce Pascoe & Bill Gammage

Adapted by Jasmin McGaughey

Illustrated by Savi Ross

First published in Australia in 2025 by Thames & Hudson Australia
Wurundjeri Country, 132A Gwynne Street, Cremorne, Victoria 3121

28 27 26 5 4 3 2

ISBN 978-1-760-76357-2
ISBN 978-1-76076-549-1 (ebook)

A catalogue record for this book is available from the National Library of Australia

Front cover: Illustration by Savi Ross, designed by Sancia Ridgeway
Design: Sancia Ridgeway
Design advisor: Andy Warren Design
Editing: Melissa-Jane Fogarty
Your turns: Cara Shipp

Printed and bound in China by C&C Offset Printing Co., Ltd

Thames & Hudson Australia wishes to acknowledge that Aboriginal and Torres Strait Islander peoples are the first storytellers of this nation and the Traditional Custodians of the land on which we live and work. We acknowledge their continuing culture and pay respect to Elders past and present.

thamesandhudson.com.au

Aboriginal and Torres Strait Islander peoples are advised that this book contains the names and images of people who have passed away.

The stories in this book are shared with the permission of the original storytellers.

Content warning:
Some of the content in this book may be confronting for some readers.

A note on language: There are a lot of different Aboriginal and Torres Strait Islander languages, words and spellings for cultural concepts and people groups. We have used the preferred words and spellings of the authors.

Contents

Welcome

Did you know there are more trees in Australia now than there were in 1788 when the British came to colonise us and take our land? How could that be, with centuries of clearing land for farms and cities, for logging and from wildfires?

Aboriginal people kept this land healthy for over 60,000 years. How did Aboriginal people do it? Aboriginal people took their custodianship of the country seriously and managed it simply by working in collaboration with nature and not trying to usurp it – to change and control it. Country provided everything people needed for tens of thousands of years.

This book will surprise you and open your eyes to new ideas. Aboriginal Country taught people how to farm without fences, using firestick farming and other clever methods. There was no need to clear the land of vegetation or introduce hard-hoofed animals that destroy Country and cause emissions. There was no need to treat native foods as pests and weeds to be eradicated.

Bruce Pascoe and Bill Gammage will show you that there is hope for the future if we look back at Aboriginal ways of working with Country, and learn from the past and current practices.

How can you care for Country?

Margo Ngawa Neale

MANDU II

Chapter 1: Personal perspectives

What do you love most about Australia? Do you know what town you were born in or where you lived when you first arrived in Australia? Maybe you have a favourite memory of famous Australian things – koalas, kangaroos, the Sydney Opera House or Uluru. There are so many wonderful animals and places in Australia.

And we have a responsibility to take care of all of them. In this book we're going to talk about lots of different ways to do just that.

From Uncle Bruce Pascoe

My name is Bruce Pascoe, and I am a writer and farmer. You might have seen my book called *Young Dark Emu*. It's a book about my research into the way First Nations people cared for Country over many thousands of years. I am a Yuin, Bunurong and Tasmanian man, and I currently live on my farm in Gippsland, Victoria.

I'll talk more about my farm later in this book. But I also wanted to talk about how we act as Australians. We have a responsibility to care for this country. There are so many things here that are important. What do you want to protect and care for in Australia?

When I was at school it was like Aboriginal Australia didn't exist. The only thing I can remember doing was colouring in a boomerang. This complete absence made me very uneasy. It didn't make sense that Aboriginal people simply left the land when asked. 'Why would they do that?' I wondered. When older Aboriginal people helped me search for my own family they were cross with me for my ignorance of the real history of Australia and I made a promise to myself, and to them, that I would try to write books which told a different story.

I am so grateful to those old people; they made me responsible for oyster, plants and wallaby. In that way they ensured that I would have to look after the water, the land and the animals. It keeps me busy, I can tell you.

From Bill Gammage

My name is Bill Gammage, and I am a historian. I grew up in Wagga Wagga in the Riverina district of New South Wales. My brother and I often used to go into the country riding our bikes, mushrooming or rabbiting or just looking.

Later on I worked on a farm, on the wheat harvest, where I saw many paddocks with big old trees but no small ones. I used to wonder what would happen when all the old trees died out. What do you think?

Later I read history books about the Riverina, and saw that early 'settlers' described grassland where dense forest is now. Why? I looked at many possible explanations, and finally found that the grassland was made by fire: not just any fire, but repeated deliberate, careful fire – Aboriginal fire, or what I call 1788 fire, from before the British first occupied Sydney Cove. Using fire was one important way in which Aboriginal people cared for their Country and all the plants and animals on it. But those new arrivals feared fire and stopped people from burning, which let trees colonise the grassland the early newcomers described. In this way in many places the land changed from being well managed to a wilderness.

Your turn

Your connections to place

- Draw or make a photo collage of your favourite plant or animal and a place you want to protect.

Exploring First Nations Countries and languages

- Whose Country are you living on? Whose Country is your school situated on? Are they the same or different? What are some features of the water, plants and animals in the Countries you research?
- Explore using the AIATSIS Map (aiatsis.gov.au) and Gambay map (gambay.com.au). Search for 'Indigenous rangers', 'Aboriginal NRM (Natural Resource Management)' or 'Torres Strait Islander NRM' in your local area.

Chapter 2:
by Bill Gammage

Before and after 1788

What did Australia look like before the Europeans invaded in 1788? It would probably surprise most of us if we got to travel back in time to see Australia then.

When the Europeans arrived, they saw big mobs of grazing animals, skies flocked with birds and waters black with fish. They could see the bottom of Sydney Harbour because the water was so clear!

Another way the land looked different was because much of it wasn't covered in thick bush. Instead, it had large areas of grassland with few trees, even where there is thick bush today.

Why has the land changed?

The land has changed so much since 1788 because the people in charge have changed. In 1788, Australia was not in its 'natural' state. Really, it had been made or carefully cared for by Aboriginal people. It was not simply land, but Country. But the newcomers essentially saw the land as a resource.

'Country' is an English word Aboriginal people have transformed. For them, Country is physical and spiritual – it is land, water, sky, habitats, places, totems and relationships. It is a world of the land and the mind, a way of believing and behaving. Creator Ancestors made Country in the Dreaming, and they still watch over it.

In the Aboriginal way of understanding, everything must be cared for. The driest corner is as much Country as the richest park. Every place is filled with presences, rights and duties, binding people for life to keeping Country alive. Some places might not be touched for years, even decades, but not for a moment do carers forget them. Far from home, people dream their Country and yearn to be part of it once more.

Dreaming cares for Country

People cared for Country via the Dreaming. The Dreaming has two basic rules: obey the Law, and leave the world as you found it. Change is normal, of course: seasons come and go, kangaroos graze grass into lawns, ants stitch leaves, kites and brown hawks drop burning sticks to start a new fire, bettong digging softens soil so plants grow.

Culture cares for Country

As a Ramingining (NT) Elder said, 'The seasons are not about the passing of time. They are about how things link together ... Everything is part of a rhythm.' The Dreaming requires all these cycles to continue as they are, so each generation of people leaves the world as they found it.

The Dreaming encourages this via totems. Everything with shape – people, Ancestors, animals, plants, stars, earth, wind, diseases, and introduced species like rabbits, camels and house flies – has a totem that comes from a Creator Ancestor.

Every totem has people who belong to it, and who must care for it. For example, an emu man must care for emus and emu habitat, and they must care for him.

Songlines are environmentally grounded. They are the tracks the Creator Ancestors followed as they made the features of the land – rivers, mountains, islands and seas. They explain and maintain a habitat and, as with the Seven Sisters and Native Cat Songlines, they show us important knowledge and story. They tie the land together. Every tiny part of land, sea and sky, every totem, is part of at least one Songline. If you'd like to learn more you can read the *Songlines* book in this series.

Fire is a totem. Fire appears in Songlines and is subject to Law, just like people. Fire and people need and help each other. Without people there would be no fire; without fire there would be no people. They work together.

What has changed?

Many Australians think the land back in 1788 looked the same as it does now, but unfortunately much has changed, especially the number of native plants and animals. In the whole world, Australia is among the countries with the most species extinctions, and the most serious land degradation. But there are ways we can work to save our species and to make our environment healthier.

Animals

What do you think is Australia's most famous animal? Perhaps the kangaroo? It's possible that populations of eastern grey kangaroos and possums have increased across the country since Europeans arrived. But many smaller marsupials have gone extinct, or are endangered.

A mala, or rufous hare-wallaby, looks like a tiny version of a kangaroo. In the central deserts of Australia, mala could be found all over the place before Europeans settled there! But after 1788 many Aboriginal people were stopped from caring for the land, and animals like the mala almost became extinct because they were forced to move off their Country or their food and shelter were not cared for. Because the land was not cared for, hot fires became more common. These hot fires then destroyed plant cover and exposed the little mala to cats and foxes, and it faced extinction.

In its home area the mala went extinct in about 1991 but is now being reintroduced from breeding sanctuaries. Many other small marsupials, such as bettongs and bilbies, are being bred in protected areas to save their species from extinction.

Other animals facing extinction are:

- koalas
- platypus
- dunnarts
- greater gliders
- bandicoots
- quolls

In the past 200 years, a third of the world's mammals made extinct have been Australian.

Since invasion in 1788, at least seventy animal species have gone extinct. This is a huge and heartbreaking number. Researchers think even more species went extinct before we even knew they existed! As well, at least 120 native animal species are now critically endangered – which means they are close to becoming extinct.

Birds

Some birds have been affected too. Inland birds like galahs, crested pigeons and little corellas have spread around the country and beyond their former inland habitats. But some offshore birds, and land birds, such as the paradise parrot, have become extinct, while ground dwelling birds, such as emus, cassowaries, mallee fowl, curlews and quail, and birds like wedge-tailed eagles, black swans, wrens and some cockatoos and parrots have shrunk their range. Some are so endangered they exist mainly in refuges.

In the 1851 Gippsland fires, two children were saved from the flames by hiding under the bodies of birds that dropped from the sky. Today, there are not enough birds even to imagine that.

Reptiles and insects

Reptile populations have also declined. Over twenty species are critically endangered. Do you know why? Mostly it's because their habitats have been destroyed by buildings or fires, but humans have also been quick to kill things they are afraid of – like snakes. Insects in general are fewer – including on car windscreens!

Soil

In many places the soil has changed a lot since 1788.

- In 1788 some topsoil was soft enough to push your finger into! Since then, topsoil has been packed tightly by our heavy vehicles and by hoofed animals like cows introduced by Europeans. Topsoil has also been blown or washed away by the weather, so tree roots that were once safely nestled underground have been exposed. Can you find such tree roots in your area?
- In large parts of inland Australia the soil is saline (salty) because it was once under the sea. Artesian (underground) water there can be salty too, but fresh water, being lighter, sits above it.
- After Europeans reached the inland, their bores, pumps and drains for mining and watering stock steadily lowered the fresh water, causing the soaks, springs and waterholes Aboriginal people depended on to dry up. This is still happening!
- Elsewhere, changes in water flow have let salt water rise, killing trees and bushes. The bigger the trees, the more fresh water they drink, so the more readily salt comes up to kill them. Giant river red gums that were healthy sixty years ago are now dead from salination.

Erosion

Erosion has removed many hectares of land since 1788. It can be caused by deep ploughing (as some farmers do) or by clearing or overgrazing native grasses. Erosion gullies are common in Australia.

Water

So much of our water in Australia has disappeared. It's a bit strange to think that a country famous for being dry and hot was once so full of water! Before the Europeans arrived, rivers ran slow and shallow because native grasses grew in all the right places. Even fast coastal streams generally ran slower in 1788. Native grasses slowed the flows, and streams choked with debris. Slow streams run shallow. Shallow streams flood easily, letting water spread and refresh more land.

The Murray River and the Darling River are big! Back around 1788, they had lots of fords – places that were crossable because they were shallow. Now, these rivers run deeper.

Even though you and I might think it's obvious to keep the water flowing in a place like Australia, this didn't happen after the Europeans settled. They cut channels of water and drained swamps, thinking that the water would always be there for them. In paddocks today, black soil or reeds can tell us where swamps once were.

Governments drain natural waterways on a big scale. For example, behind the Coorong in South Australia, there is so much more dry land than there was in 1788. This means there are fewer summer-saving wetlands and fewer refuges from drought and fire for animals.

Grass

Grass was central to healthy Country in 1788. Grassland carried many useful plants and was home to most big animals. It was a firebreak, it made seeing and travelling easier, and it confined forest, making forest resources more predictable.

These days native grasses like kangaroo, wallaby, spear, poa and millet are less common. These important grasses are dormant in the winter and in the summer ripen. Thus they shield the land from drought and provide feed in the seasons where feed is now hardest to find. Today's introduced crops and weeds tend to be green in winter and dead in summer. The changes to plants and grasses has changed the summer colour of Australia from the tan native grasses to the creamy white of introduced species.

Grassland provides food and shelter not just for people but for many plants and animals, so we need to take care with how and where grass is grown. To help care for Country today, a National Grass Day would make as much sense as our National Tree Day!

Kangaroo grass was common in 1788. For most of the year, it's a grey-green colour. In summer it keeps soil damp, protecting the ground from drought, and it offers feed to animals like kangaroos when they really need it. When kangaroo grass is burnt it grows back easily. In fact, kangaroo grass needs a refreshing fire about every two to four years. The complete opposite to this is Mitchell grass, which grows in the north of Australia. Mitchell grass doesn't like frequent burning!

Trees

Have you heard of National Tree Day? It's a day when people are encouraged to plant new trees. This is very worthwhile, as some areas have lost trees, yet overall there may be more trees now than there were before the Europeans arrived. Places thick with trees today were grassland in 1788.

The way our forests grow has changed over the years. A forest is more than just trees. It also grows what we call an understorey or scrub. An understorey is the scrub that builds up under bigger plants. It is a fire fuse and helps flames lift up high. The understorey makes the forest look thick and closed off. In 1788, much more forest was open, without an understorey. This protected against big fires, and provided habitats for grassland plants and animals. Yet there was always some scrub, because it is a habitat too!

Grandfather trees are big and very old. These days it's common to see dense groups of young eucalypt trees growing straight up, often with hardly any big old grandfather trees in sight. The younger trees are dense because the seedlings have not been thinned by fire, and they grow straight because they must race each other for light.

Much forest was open in 1788. Horses and wagons could pass easily, and early travellers wrote of walking distances in times and places Olympic marathoners could not match now because the bush is much thicker. Today we are so used to a scrubby understorey that we think it was always there.

What now?

Think about all the changes that have happened in Australia. The soil and the waterways have changed, and many native animals, birds, insects, grasses and trees are no longer here, while many are struggling to survive.

What do you think the future holds for Australians? What type of future do you want to see when you think about our animals, grasses, trees and seas?

There are lots of things we could learn from how Aboriginal people cared for Country, and still do. Learning from the past could help us make sure the future of our land, seas and animals is safe and healthy.

Your turn

Caring for Country

- Select a 'natural thing with shape', something that might be a totem: a species of bird, reptile, insect or mammal, a spring, well or river, a species of plant or tree, or fire. Research your chosen natural thing: where is it found? How does it survive? What is needed to care for it? Is it endangered (and how)? What can be done to regenerate it? How do First Nations people care for it?
- Consider how First Nations people managed the land through their totems. Each person was given a totem to care for (a 'natural thing with shape'). Consider this example problem: the kangaroos have eaten too much native grass in one spot. There is no grass left and now the parrots have no seeds to eat and the lizards have no home. The kangaroos need to move to another eating place and the spot needs some help to regenerate new native grass. The people who have kangaroos, parrots, lizards and grass as their totems will need to talk with each other to discuss a solution. What could they do?

Chapter 3:
by Bruce Pascoe
Land care

Fear of the land

Many Australians are taught to fear our country. There are spiders, sharks and snakes just lying in wait to get us! Some say the land here is so harsh and dangerous that it's best for us to live close to the coast.

I think fearing land and what lives here is an idea born from the first European invaders who thought they had to conquer the country. They thought they had to force the country to change into something like the places they'd left in Europe.

I don't want to get bitten by a snake either but I was taught by my father to be calm when I see one. We lived on King Island when I was about eight and it is the snakiest place on earth. Dad taught me to walk around behind them, not to get between them and where they were heading. 'Don't flap your arms around, just move quietly. The snake is more scared of you than you are of him.'

My mother taught me to love all things. She didn't approve when I collected birds' eggs. I wanted to see them hatch but of course without their mother's warmth they couldn't. Mum taught me those things and one day I was sheltering from the rain under a boxthorn bush and a blue wren started to pull the loose threads from the cuffs of my jeans and take them to the nest she was building. It seemed to go on for hours and the bond between me and that bird has stayed with me since that rainy day.

Being afraid of Australia probably led people to think of the wildlife and the trees as their enemies. They thought chopping down trees would show others how hardworking they were. Lots of people and religions have seen the world as something to take, own and control. This attitude has made our forests around the whole world shrink.

Did you know that before the 1970s and 1980s whales almost became extinct? It took the determination of people we called hippies to protest and put a stop to it. They saved the whales.

But who is saving the trees?

Commercial forests and fire

Do you remember the summer fires in 2019 and 2020? We have called it Black Summer. The east coast of Australia suffered from terrible bushfires and most of these fires were made worse by commercial forests. The small-tree commercial forests were created by humans growing and cutting down trees to make timber.

These types of forests are not natural to the real Australian wilderness. We need timber for our houses but we must be careful about how many trees we use and how much timber we waste.

Commercial forests are planned and created by humans. Usually, they're full of the same sized trees growing closely together, which can lead to fire spreading quickly through them. In the 2019–20 fires, commercial forests and some unmanaged national parks were full of fuel loads. Fuel loads are scrub, leaves and trees that ignite and can cause an inferno.

Before the Europeans invaded, forests in Australia looked completely different. They would have maybe ten to twelve trees each acre and there would have been many more big grandfather trees. Massive trees were never close enough to touch each other. First Nations people maintained forests as places to grow grass and vegetables, allow animals to graze and allow for easier travel. Fire in these kinds of forests was controllable.

Unfortunately, today it would be hard to find these types of original forests. Now we use so much packaging and paper that forests are mostly considered for commercial reasons only. It has meant that our forests are not properly controlled, and we live in danger if we live near them.

During the 2019–2020 fires I was living on a property near Mallacoota, in Victoria. Once the massive fires had lessened, my neighbours and I made our way to our farms and houses and fought off the local fires still threatening our homes.

Killer trees

When driving alongside forests have you ever seen marks spraypainted onto trees? Sometimes you can find a big letter 'K' on the side of a tree. What do you think the 'K' stands for? The 'K' doesn't mean killer fire, or killer forestry or killer forest management. It means killer tree. That 'K' blames fires on the trees. In the summer fires of 2019–20 I saw some of these Ks painted on the trees near my home. Thousands of these trees were destroyed because people thought big trees were the problem. In fact it's too many small trees that cause wildfires.

The most ancient trees seem to suffer the worst once marked as a 'killer tree'. This includes one scar tree (scar trees are trees where sections of bark have been removed to make a canoe or coolamon) where my uncle was made to sleep to prove to his grandfather that he was ready for the lore. That tree was massive, and the hollow section at its base was large enough for two people to sleep. It had five large windows in the trunk that had been made by Dooligah to express the power of the lore. Dooligah is a spirit who inhabits the forest and his job is to make sure people behave and are well and not violent, greedy or disrespectful. People today are frightened of Dooligah, but he only upholds the lore; he is not committing casual violence. That was the old grandfather's message: uphold your lore. We begged Parks Victoria to look after this tree a year before the fires exploded, but in the aftermath the Dooligah tree was cut down. It didn't burn, couldn't have burnt, but it was cut down and other trees were destroyed too, because they were also 'killer trees'.

Natural wilderness

If we all learnt to nurture Australia's natural forests, it could help us all live safely for many generations. Our forests did that for around 120,000 years before invasion.

Wilderness wasn't a concept Aboriginal people knew before the Europeans invaded. First Nations people visited and used every corner of the land. They worked with the land in a type of close communication.

But what would a natural forest managed by First Nations peoples look like, and how would it be treated?

- It would have fewer but larger trees per acre.
- We would harvest trees for timber but without wasting it. We wouldn't turn the perfect timber into woodchips, send it to Japan for processing and then buy it back as packaging for our hamburgers.
- We would respect the trees we harvest by paying for their true value.
- We wouldn't cut trees and leave the forest floor in a mess of stumps and soil. When we do this the next crop is skinnier than the one before it.

All in all, it's about managing our forests sustainably so that our grandchildren (you kids reading this book) can have forests too.

I will talk later about our farm, Yumburra, where we are growing the traditional Aboriginal foods and also trying to return the forest to the way it was when Lieutenant Cook arrived. Many other farmers are interested in making the forests less flammable and more useful to people.

Early European explorers described the land they saw at the beginning of the invasion as lush and open, pleasant and gentle. In those days there were fewer trees and small plants on the forest floor. The Europeans called it grass but mostly it was our root vegetables, such as the yam daisy and chocolate lily. There were no fences, apart from those used for game drives (herding animals to eat), because the land didn't belong to individuals; it was gifted to language groups and clans so that they would care for it, not exploit it.

Aboriginal and Torres Strait Islander care for Country has been interrupted by the government. After 1788, First Nations people weren't allowed to care for their Country the way they had for many years, and so Australians began to see tangled undergrowth as normal. Timber operations removed bigger trees and made way for more undergrowth and scrub. But this undergrowth can catch alight very quickly.

A number of people from the local Aboriginal community work on our farm, Yumburra. We want to grow ancestral grasses and tubers (a kind of root) so that our people can take part in the Aboriginal food market. After the Black Summer, Mother Earth invited us into the forest, and we saw her recovery. The tree ferns were first, shooting up as a bright- green celebration against a background of ash and char. Electric-green shoots appeared on the eucalypts; bronze, pink and scarlet colour licked at the blackened trunks. Later the wattles and kangaroo apples sprang up from seed they had cast after the blaze.

We looked for seedlings to use to rebuild burnt areas and care for others. The forest floor was full of ironbarks, peppermints, hickory wattles, casuarinas, cherries and brave maidenhairs.

We had removed cattle from the farm before the fires to let the soil rest. When the fires came they burnt a lot of trees and grass but they also killed some weeds, which gave our fire-resistant plants a chance to flourish. For example, we were able to harvest three types of grasses after the fires. We found garrara ngalluk (spear grass), buru ngalluk (kangaroo grass) and a lot of mamadjan ngalluk (dancing grass); all of these grasses were used by our old people to produce flour.

Changing our thinking about farming

What do you think we could change about how we farm in Australia?

There are some farmers who use tractors that are directed by satellites in the sky. They've pulled down fences between properties so that the huge machines can harvest in straight lines over hundreds of kilometres. This is really beneficial to them. I think there are some other new ways to farm that could help us out too.

Our grasses are perennial so there is no need to plough the land and our grasses need no fertiliser, pesticide or irrigation – a huge benefit to the environment.

Did you know there were many bandicoots and potoroos in the forests before colonisation in Australia? But most of them have disappeared because of the way we use the land (and because of the introduction of foxes and cats into the Australian wildlife).

Farming solutions

Issue	Idea
Drought costs our government millions of dollars.	We could restart growing plants that are less water-hungry.
Blue-green algae is caused by artificial fertilisers being washed off farms into the river and too much water being used for irrigation, which makes the river's water temperature rise. This kills fish in the Murray-Darling Basin every year.	We could move away from crops like rice and cotton, which require a lot of water and fertiliser. Both these things help kill fish in the Murray-Darling.
Australia, like most countries, is struggling to reduce carbon emissions.	Aboriginal food plants like kangaroo grass and chocolate lily are perennial (they do not have to be replanted) so they hold carbon in the soil and reduce greenhouse gases.

Are there any other ideas you can think of?

Farming, hunting and gathering

Aboriginal and Torres Strait Islander peoples had and continue to have many ways to grow, cultivate, harvest and maintain crops, grasses and other plant foods as well as meat from animals and fish. Many of the Europeans who came to Australia didn't recognise this, because the First Nations methods didn't look like European methods.

At Yumburra we were thrilled to see Indigenous grasses come back to the forest. It means we're closer to returning the forest on our farm to one where big trees and food grasses dominate. This doesn't mean we will lose our wattles and grevilleas, indigoferas and hakeas, but we'll end up with a productive and far less flammable forest.

We want to remove the smaller eucalypts from our farm's forest lands and sell the timber as sawlogs. We have already used a lot of this timber to build fences and sheds on the farm.

It's a slow process and won't be achieved overnight, but we are trying to reverse the poor land management decisions of the past 230 years.

We are lucky to have an Aboriginal engineer and steel fabricator in our community. Hopefully, after we have designed our next, bigger harvester, he will build it for us. We want to make sure there are more Aboriginal and Torres Strait Islander people in the engineering field.

Hunting and gathering for food and resources is only one farming method used by First Nations people in Australia. We also farmed and gardened – not in the same way as Europeans, but why should we? Europe is very far from Australia and a completely different environment.

Did you know Aboriginal people were known to select seed and carry it in small cone baskets hanging from their necks so that they could trade or gift it to neighbouring clans?

It's a very sad history that prevented Aboriginal and Torres Strait Islander peoples from keeping up this type of land care. There were many massacres and killings of First Nations people by the Europeans after 1788. It became too dangerous for First Nations people to be out in the open. This level of murder and intimidation lasted well into the 20th century across all the states. It was horrible to see in *The Guardian* a photograph of Aboriginal men chained by the neck for resisting the law of the invaders. They were chained to a tree and left out in the sun for days. These chains were still being used in the 1960s.

What could the future look like?

Now that people are learning what our forests need we can create a place where all the birds, insects and animals can flourish, and where the koalas and wallabies will never have their pads burnt off in uncontrolled fire. It will be a different forest from the one we see today, but Australia has experienced this forest type before, during the many years of Aboriginal forest management.

Your turn

The land and you

- Uncle Bruce tells the story of the blue wren who tore cotton from his jeans. He feels he always has a connection to that little bird. Do you have a connection story about a plant or animal you came across out in the wild?
- Uncle Bruce asks, 'Who is saving the trees?' What ideas do you have for saving trees in our environment? Have you ever volunteered to help this cause?
- Uncle Bruce tells us about an important tree where his people would go to learn the lore from one of their creator spirits, Dooligah. Are there any scar trees or significant sites in your local area? Research this and/or ask your local First Nations rangers/NRM (Natural Resource Management). If you find a special site, is it protected by the government? Do you think it should be?

The land and First Nations people

- Draw your impressions of an Australian landscape before and after 1788 in two side-by-side pictures, using the way Uncle Bruce describes traditional land (pp. 38–41). Label the main differences between the two pictures. Can you describe how First Nations people work with the land instead of against it? What are the differences in First Nations ways of caring for land and the early colonisers approach and attitudes?

Chapter 4: by Bill Gammage
The role of fire

How Australians think about fire

What is the first thing you think of when you read the word 'fire'? Some people think about cooking sausages or fish over a camp fire. In Australia, most people are terrified of fire. It's important to know that fire is dangerous, but if we get too scared of it, we won't be able to use it for our benefit.

Fire and humans have shared a special alliance for a long time. In Australia, Aboriginal people studied fire as children, and if their totem was fire, they devoted their whole lives to it. Can you imagine devoting your life to one thing?

Fire was a tool to manage Country. Burning areas of Country could help Aboriginal people keep their world diverse, tame the areas of the land more likely to go up in flames, and help things grow. I call this giving the land the kiss of life.

Using fire to care for Country was always planned. It was guided by experts, Ancestors and neighbours. They would consider three main questions:

1. What would be burnt?
2. When would it be burnt?
3. How would it be burnt?

Burning started with ceremonies. The correct rituals had to be done at the right time by the right people.

Aboriginal people burnt the *most* useful land *most* often. They might not burn sensitive land for generations. But no land was uncared for in 1788 – newcomers brought that.

People used many different fires to look after Country, for example:

Photograph of cool fire

Photograph of hot fire

Cool fires

Cool fires are lit on purpose where there is little fuel (like grass, bushes or trees) and damp or cool conditions. The flames are always low, sometimes so low that you can step over them. Cool fires don't ignite shrubs or trees. They are lit to help protect camps and special places and reduce fuel, and refresh plants that need fire to flourish.

Cool fires used to cover a lot of land. At specific times of the year, cool and frequent fire is used on long grass, scrub, tree-packed areas and rocky hills. It can create fire breaks and it's a good method for fire farming too! Fire farming is to farm animals with fire, just as if they were in a paddock. I'll say more about fire farming later.

Hot fires

Hot fire has high flames like you see on TV. Aboriginal people used cool fires to stop fuel building up for hot fires. They used hot fires rarely, but these can help clean up Country that is dirty or overrun with weeds, or help clear trees and stop scrub germinating.

Unplanned fire

These fires are dangerous as it's difficult to contain or control them. Unplanned fires before 1788 might have started by lightning or because of war.

Backburning

This involves carefully starting fires on purpose so that the ground becomes burnt. The burnt land has no fuel, so it will stop a big bushfire if it comes along.

Patch burn

This type of fire burns Country in patches or mosaics so that some unburnt land is left as feed and shelter for animals, birds and reptiles. This was a common fire used in 1788 and is still used today.

Sheet burn

People light sheet burns on long stretches of dry country in the morning or at dusk. These fires are aimed at big unburnt patches. In the north they are lit in the late dry season. They burn off large areas, usually grassland.

How did Aboriginal people care for Country?

Protecting

Aboriginal people protected plants from unsuitable fires by backburning around them. This careful burning would create a ring of safety where newer, hotter fire would not be able to pass. Spirits might live in such places and can blind people with smoke if they light a fire too close to a special place.

Aboriginal people had to know a lot about fire. For example:

- In Tasmania, fire kills species like beech, King Billy pine and pencil pine, yet 2000-year-old trees of these species have flourished even with fire in use around them.
- In the centre of Australia, native bees prefer desert bloodwood, so people take care not to let flames or smoke damage the flowers of this tree.

Aboriginal people also had to know the difference between cool fire and hot fire. They knew cool fire prevented hot fires and wouldn't damage flowers, fruit, nuts and seed.

Protecting plants required balance. Sometimes people would have to choose whether to burn grass to find yams or wait until the same grass turned into grain. In wet country, people preferred the yams; in dry country people preferred the grain because yams won't grow where it's too dry.

Safeguarding

Helping plants and animals was a major responsibility. From rainforest to spinifex plains, plants were patch burnt to ensure a variety of safe habitats and a land full of different living things.

'Fireweeds' (flammable plants) like bush tobacco (pituri) and some desert raisin (*Solanum* species) might grow near fire-sensitive mulga and fire-dependent spinifex. Only 'fire' or 'no fire' at the exact right time could balance such diverse plants.

People helped some plants by destroying competition. Cycad nuts (*Zamia* species) are poisonous: eating them raw can kill someone! But once the poison is taken out, by pounding and washing, the nuts are highly nutritious, so Aboriginal people made cycad gardens. They burnt away competing plants and timed their fires to help the nuts grow in a way they could predict. They would gather the nuts for ceremony.

Firestick farming

Aboriginal people used fire to farm animals. By managing Country with strategic burning they created areas where hunting was made easier. A good example is firestick farming to harvest kangaroos. Kangaroos can smell sweet, fresh grass that grows after a cool fire from a long way off. To fire farm them you must ensure that they go where you've burnt. So you must make sure the grass you burn is the sweetest and most nutritious available, with shelter nearby so kangaroos won't feel vulnerable.

The best grass is on the best soil. Trees grow there, so you must burn to keep the land clear. But you also have to leave some trees as shelter, so kangaroos don't feel too exposed. Not too much, though! We wouldn't want the kangaroos to feel like they would be slowed down by the trees. It's all a delicate balance.

Aboriginal people used fire to care for Country. They would backburn around camps or single trees to protect them from hotter fire, or sheetburn to clean Country, or hotburn to help create scrub to shelter small birds. Sometimes they chose not to burn, to make forest or protect a vulnerable species.

Refreshing

Caring for plants meant not only making sure the plants grew, but also that they grew in healthy ways.

Do you know what a lerp is? I reckon not many people in Australia do!

A lerp is an insect that lives in the south of Australia on certain mallee and gum trees. Lerps make a sweet, sugary manna, and people burnt their trees to promote fresh leaves to feed the lerps, then harvested the manna the next year. This is one type of refreshing.

Before invasion, Aboriginal people refreshed entire plant communities by moving them with fire!

In Tasmania, they used westerlies (winds blowing from the west) to drive fires into rainforest, clearing it to make grass. But they did not want grass plains too big, nor to destroy too much eucalypt, so they also used no fire as a tool, taking care to leave the western eucalypt edge unburnt. This let eucalypts regenerate and move east, then let rainforest follow under their shelter to reclaim the ground. So grass, eucalypts and rainforest followed each other across the ground, each being refreshed on new land.

Balancing

Animals were culled (killed) if their numbers got too large outside their totem places. Sometimes kangaroos were driven over cliffs to keep their numbers balanced. If animals became too few, people banned hunting them or damaging their habitat.

People also thinned or cleared trees for grass. They removed the scrub and burnt grass to reveal food plants. They would turn rainforest into grassland! These days, much of this is rainforest again.

Insects were also suppressed by fire. Do you find buzzing insects annoying sometimes? Well, good fire practice kept swarms of insects away from grain. Farmers today struggle with insects eating their crops, but Aboriginal peoples used fire to control things like this. Fire can reduce leeches, insects, mosquitoes and ticks.

Distributing

Fire and no fire allowed Aboriginal people to spread plants within their Country easily. They could decide where things grew. Locating plants helped distribute the animals that ate them, and in turn their predators. This type of thinking made everything balanced and predictable.

Animals are always attracted to things they prefer. Kangaroos crowd onto golf greens to graze delicious grass. They don't need to, they prefer to. Koalas prefer freshly grown leaf tips, so fire can lure them to newly sprouting eucalypts. Possums also prefer fresh tips, so they move easily from unburnt parks to green backyards. Most animals prefer a special kind of shelter: euros like rocky hills, koalas prefer tall eucalypts, scrub wallabies and small birds go for thick growth. People made Country to suit every plant, animal, bird, reptile and insect.

Two golden rules for caring for Country:

1. Every species must be helped to grow while being balanced with other species, including humans! The world was not made just for people. That's the point of totems: they create specialists in understanding and protecting a species and its habitat.

2. Fire is an ally but must be managed. It is hard work, but it was work done regularly before invasion. No matter what the local conditions, people everywhere worked with fire and no fire to live on and care for Country.

All this burning led many Aboriginal people to move around a lot so that all the land was cared for. Often they moved even if they had plenty of food and shelter.

Fire language

Fire and burning was so important that language groups had many different words and phrases to talk about it easily.

Yanyuwa people have single words for several fire concepts: ngarrki, 'badly burnt Country', warrman, 'well-burnt Country, good to hunt on' and rumalumarrinjerra, 'lighting small fires in a row, to burn a beach front or a large plain'.

West Arnhem people have the phrases anbirlu yahwurd for 'low, creeping fires' and arni wurlhge for 'cleaning the Country' with hot fires.

East of Perth in the 1830s people had a different word for every stage of a burn.

Arnhem Land plateau people link bushfire, the peak fire season, and in some dialects burnable grass with the same stem word, wurrk.

Martu people say nyurnma for a freshly burnt area, waru-waru for the green-shoot time after fire, mukura for the growth flush one to three years later, and mangul when spinifex begins to dominate Country five to seven years later.

None of these words have an English version and none of these words describe random fire. What do you think about that?

The basic purposes of fire and no fire were and are the same: to make sure Country has lots of different types of plants and animals, and to help regulate these plant and animal populations. To leave the world as the Ancestors made it.

Controlling

Whoever lit a fire, even a campfire, was responsible for it. Random fire was never allowed. Random fire made animals move in ways that were hard to predict. The animals couldn't fight against fire – they could only run or try to hide underground. All of today's big bushfires are random fires.

The key parts of controlling fire are frequency, timing (year, season, day), intensity and patchiness. To control fire, Aboriginal people would burn coolly and in patches. They knew when the grass would be all damp with dew and which way the wind would blow. They aimed their fire at water or rock or burnt ground to make sure it would stop. They kept careful watch along the edges of the fire and used the wind to make the fire turn back on itself without spreading further.

Uluru Elders have explained how connected fire and Country are:

Country is not burnt in just any way. Aṉungu [Aṉangu] are taught by their grandparents the proper way to burn, according to the Tjukurpa [Dreaming]. Certain places, such as sacred sites and trees, such as fig trees, should not be burnt because of their associations with the Tjukurpa. The area around these sites and trees is often burnt to protect them, and show others that the land is being properly cared for.

Fire farming today

How might we use Aboriginal fire farming today? Aboriginal knowledge of Country and understanding how to read the weather is crucial to fire farming. There are also different reasons to burn so it's important to know why each area is being burnt. For example, grass, yams and orchids can all share Country, but their fire frequency and timing differs. Burning is a big job and we need to make sure we talk with everyone involved.

An important part of fire farming would be backburning vulnerable places. Backburning protects fire-sensitive plants, ceremony sites, conservation reserves, camps and water frontages. These are usually burnt early in the morning, when ground and plants are still damp.

We need to choose what day to start fire farming. Locally, First Nations peoples know when a time to burn is coming. They know this because they know the season and they notice the way grass feels.

We also need to choose what type of fire to use and what pattern to burn in. Occasionally hot fire is needed. Hot fire can be used to kill off melaleuca scrub or push back wet forest or clean up Country. But a whole lifetime might pass without a hot fire being lit. Cool fires are much easier to control. They trickle over the ground, make only white smoke, don't throw embers or damage tree canopies. Cool fires give animals time to escape, leave bigger unburnt patches, don't germinate scrub, don't bake the soil or its creatures, and leave some leaf litter unburnt. Cool fires don't leave the ground completely bare.

Examples to break up or slow down a fire to make it cool are:

- burning into the wind;
- burning into obstacles such as water, rock, cliffs or burnt ground;
- burning downhill;
- burning when plants and ground are damp or wet;
- directing the flame front by choking it off at the sides.

Most importantly, we need to start as soon as possible to work with fire before random fire damages more of our country.

Your turn

Connecting with fire

- Choose an animal or plant species and research it. In what ways would fire help your animal or plant? Which kind of fire (cool, hot, backburning, patch burn, sheetburn, no fire)?
- Can you see how fire is connected in so many ways to your different chosen natural thing and display it on a poster? How does this show us that fire is an ally to be respected and worked with?

Understanding First Nations' uses of fire

- Learn more about Aboriginal uses of, and perspectives on, fire. Firesticks Alliance – an initiative established by Victor Steffensen, a prominent Tagalaka man from Far North Queensland and fire expert – is working with First Nations communities across Australia to re-incorporate traditional fire practices into caring for Country. Find out more through his resources at firesticks.org.au/resources/
- What does it mean when we say that Aboriginal people are fire farmers?

Chapter 5:
by Bill Gammage

A fire-friendly country

Australia is a continent with lots of famous animals. We're very lucky to have such a variety of land, waters and wildlife here. But how can we take better care of it all? Learning more about how Aboriginal people took care of the land before the Europeans invaded is a good place to start!

Friendly fire

As we saw in the previous chapter, Aboriginal peoples were fire farmers. In some areas they still are. Fire farming helped Aboriginal peoples hunt animals for food. With fire they made the food and shelter each animal preferred. For example, they burnt a patch of grass so that young sweet grass would regrow. Kangaroos can smell this and are lured to the patch, where people could hunt them. They made sure all the different species got to grow or live on the ground each preferred. These days we'd call this method paddocks without fences!

All this careful farming was planned – it wasn't just luck. But to the newcomers, the Europeans, this policy didn't make sense. They could not see its advantages. They wondered: how could fire help people live safely in Australia?

What they didn't know was that about 70 per cent of Australia's plants either use fire to reseed or regenerate, or otherwise recover quickly from most fires. The plants that need no fire are usually found in rainforest or wetland where fire struggles to start.

Eucalyptus trees are some of the best known trees in Australia. We know that they smell wonderful and that koalas love to eat their leaves. But did you know that eucalypts also work with fire in a strange way?

Their open branches, which never offer much shade to us humans, help channel flames up and out. Their leaves are full of oils and burn easily.

You can probably smell that oil best on a hot day because heat releases it into the world. As well, how much bark a tree drops depends on the species, but generally the bigger the tree the more bark it drops. The bark burns well. This helps regulate a fire – we can see how big the flames may get depending on how much fuel (bark and leaves) is dropped.

Eucalypt trunks resist fire unless it is very hot. After a fire has passed, trunks and branches sprout leaves again. Have you seen this? We call this new growth 'beards'. Have you see why?

There are different kinds of eucalyptus trees. Tropical eucalypts don't like fire as much as southern eucalypts. In the tropics, the eucalypts don't drop flammable oily leaves. They don't hold onto their seeds the same way as the southern eucalypts do to regrow after fire. Do you think it's strange how trees that are the same species can be so different depending on where they grow?

Fire works well with other Australian plants too. Banksias, callistemons (bottlebrush), hakeas and acacias (wattles) can grow quickly and spread seeds quickly. Fire might kill them, but it also opens their hard pods so their seeds can be spread and regrow. The ash beds made by the fire are full of nutrients to help these plants thrive. If there isn't enough fire, other plants can smother these seedlings and it will be hard for them to grow.

Types of Fire Plants		
Plant category	**Quick facts**	**Examples**
Fire Tolerant	70 per cent of Australia's plants	Southern acacias Saltbush Bluebush Emu bush *Dianella* species
Fire Dependent	Some of these plants can be found in the hottest and coldest parts of Australia.	Many scrub plants Spinifex Buttongrass Some banksia Grass trees Orchids
Fire Promoting		Many eucalypts Many scrub species, such as banksias
Fire Sensitive	Killed by fire BUT reseed after it. This means they grow again after fire.	Mulga and many other acacias
Fire Intolerant	Killed by fire completely	Many rainforest plants

Plant neighbours

Did you know that plants in different categories can be neighbours? Before the Europeans arrived, Aboriginal people carefully considered where to make plants grow.

Sometimes, plants were completely opposite to their neighbouring plants in how they responded to fire! A fire tolerant plant (a plant that didn't mind fire) grew next to a fire intolerant plant (a plant that fire killed). For example:

- Grass burnt regularly grew beside rainforests that were almost never burnt.
- Blue cypress needs cool fire every two to eight years. Any more than this or any hotter than cool fire, and it died. Yet it could be found next to fire-welcoming species.
- Desert raisin (*Solanum* species) dies without fire as it's fire dependent, but nearby foods could be either fire tolerant (bush banana, bush plum) or intolerant.
- Mulga and gidgee died even in cool fire, yet both grew among spinifex, which needed fire every three to five years to flourish.
- In heathland, where there is lots of shrubs, too much fire would create sedgeland, which is like wetland. Yet if there wasn't much fire in heathland, then woodland could be created.
- Heath banksia (*Banksia ericifolia*) needs fire to begin growing but may die if burnt more than every eight to ten years and killed if burnt every three to four years.

Fire frequency and timing

Aboriginal people carefully chose when and where to light fires, but they burnt often. The marks of fire were so common in 1788 that the Europeans thought that Aboriginal people burnt fire everywhere and all the time.

But fires were lit when the plants preferred it. It might be twice a year or every three to four years, or not for generations.

Here are some examples:

- Tree seedlings and the edges of rainforests were burnt once every one to four years.
- Scrub was burnt every three to five years (to control it) and every ten to twenty-five years to help it grow even more.
- Grass clearings in high altitude forests were probably burnt every five to seven years.
- Coastal areas were burnt every five to twenty years, depending on the plants.
- Wet eucalypt forests and rainforests were burnt sometimes decades or centuries apart!
- Grass varied a lot. Sometimes it was burnt twice a year. In other areas it was burnt once every one to four years or longer.

Basically, lots of ground was burnt compared to what the Europeans were used to. And lots more of our country was cared for by fire before invasion than it is now.

Infrequent fire usually helped trees and scrub; frequent fire helped to grow grass.

Season

When do you think is the best time of year to burn? Choosing the right seasons was crucial to fire farming.

The best time to burn is before rain. When fire comes just before rain it helps grow grass, fruits and seeds, and it helps animals breeding as there is more food for them to eat.

To predict the rain, Aboriginal people watched animals. Ants moving their eggs to high ground and birds looking for shelter were signs that the rain would soon come. You can also smell rain coming.

The next best time to burn is after rain.

Aboriginal people didn't usually burn in springtime because fire during this time would threaten young plants and baby animals and birds, and was a good time to hunt kangaroos and emus which flee from fire. People often lit fires in summer, on light fuel loads. We wouldn't dare do that today because we have let fuel build up. In northern Australia people, of course, burn in the dry season!

Day

It was also important to choose the right day and the right time of day to burn. This depended on lots of things, like the weather, the plants and animals and the ground. For example, before lighting a fire people judge how much dew is needed to put it out, then light the fire only after two or three dews have fallen. This is very local knowledge.

You can tell by feel if it's time to burn some grasses. If the grass feels powdery it will collapse under the flame and a fire will stutter out or travel slowly. If the grass stems are juicy the fire will get going slowly. If the stems snap, they're right to burn.

Intensity

We've talked about hot and cool fires, but did you know that you can control how intense a fire gets? I reckon there are a fair few people who don't realise this. Fire frequency and intensity work very closely together.

Frequent fires are cool fires and are the most important type. They don't destroy as much as hot fires and they work to help plants grow and spread food near shelters.

On Cape York, Kuku Thaypan Elders warn that a fire that scorches canopies kills flowers, reducing seeds, nectar and pollen for insects. This is harmful for birds and small marsupials and bats that eat nectar.

Hot fires weren't as common as cool fires, but sometimes they were needed. Hot fires helped scrub regenerate. Hot fires helped clean Country.

People feel joy at well-burnt Country. Central Arnhem Land Elder Dean Yibarbuk said that fire 'brings the land alive again'. He said that, 'When we do burning the whole land comes alive again – it is reborn.'

Your turn

The right time and way to burn

- How much time and effort would maintaining all the local plants and animals with fire take if we were to do it as Aboriginal people have done traditionally? Should the government employ people to do this work specifically?
- Can you see why fire management of the land was a priority for First Nations people before 1788? Can you see why time and energy may not have been spent on building structures such as homes, shops, roads and other things that Europeans focus on?

Taking climate action

- One way governments try to address climate change is by reducing Australia's carbon emissions. Research how traditional Aboriginal fire management practices can help to reduce carbon emissions. One article by Nature Conservancy Australia, 'Fighting Fire with Fire' (2023), tells us that registered Aboriginal fire projects in 2012 reduced carbon emissions by one million tonnes per year: natureaustralia.org.au
- Using your research, write a letter to your local politician asking them to consider Aboriginal fire management as a climate change and carbon emissions solution in their government policies.

Chapter 6: by Bruce Pascoe

Working with Country

Working with what we have

There are many problems in Australia's environment that we, as those who live here, should work on fixing. We also have the potential to use and grow amazing natural resources that many other countries around the world don't have.

Australian soils are different. Our soils are low in phosphorus (a nautral element that helps plants grow) but our plants adapted. European plants needed expensive superphosphate fertiliser to grow here. Our native plants have had millions of years to adapt to our soil. Why don't we use this fact for our benefit rather than trying to change the landscape by adding chemical fertilisers? Let's grow Australian plants in Australia.

There are many nutritional plants in the forests that were maintained by Aboriginal and Torres Strait Islander peoples before invasion. So maybe we need to change our ways of farming to a style that was used before the Europeans arrived in 1788?

Who owns this farming knowledge?

Intellectual property basically means ideas and information that belong to the person or people who created it. The Aboriginal and Torres Strait Islander methods of caring for plants sustainably should be recognised as knowledge created by Aboriginal and Torres Strait Islander people.

Restaurants and stores love native Australian foods, but most don't know how to include Aboriginal and Torres Strait Islander people in the benefits of foods that have been grown and harvested for many years by Aboriginal and Torres Strait Islander people.

How do you think First Nations people should be recognised for their knowledge on growing Australian plants?

The challenge for Australia is to go beyond a warm and fuzzy attitude about eating First Nations foods. We must be sure that land and social justice be extended to Aboriginal and Torres Strait Islander peoples before we accept the financial and environmental benefits of their crops. I like to say, 'You can't eat our food if you can't swallow our history.'

LANDBACK
PAY IT FORWARD

At Yumburra farm, Black Duck Foods grows traditional foods and employs Aboriginal people. We want to show people that we can grow the foods, find a market for them and give employment to our people. We have already developed a recipe to make a pesto using our warrigal greens and a preserved samphire (a swamp plant) that we simply pick from our paddocks and swamps!

Our grains can be made into flour so that we can bake breads. Once the cattle were removed from the land at Yumburra farm a whole host of useful vegetables returned. There are weeds as well, but with careful use of fire we are managing to control those.

Some of our useful plants

When the Europeans invaded Australia, they found an abundance of plant life. But they didn't always understand that this plant life was often cared for and managed by First Nations people.

In Western Australia, Lieutenant George Grey found himself among warran (yam) grounds that stretched to the horizon! Thomas Mitchell rode through over 14 kilometres of grain around the Barwon River in the New South Wales/Queensland border region. The hillsides of Melbourne were covered with yam terraces. But this clever farming wasn't credited to the First Nations people.

Here are some Aboriginal and Torres Strait Islander plants that have been used and can still be used as delicious food.

Cumbungi (or ngurun) and water ribbon

Cumbungi grows tall near water.

A long time ago when the Europeans were riding around Australia, two of them, James Kirby and Peter Beveridge, came across big stacks of cumbungi leaves. They were amazed! The stacks were as big as a house. Aboriginal people used a substance called starch from the leaves to make flour. I've also tasted this plant in a salad, and it is delicious.

At the moment, farmers are spending millions of dollars to get rid of it from canals and swamps. But why not use it for food?

The Macquarie marshes in New South Wales have lots of cumbungi. These marshes were managed by Aboriginal people before invasion and by allowing them to be grazed by cattle now we are losing a very important food source. The local Wailwan people burnt the marshes in a mosaic pattern to help the plants grow but also let animals move safely. We might need to rethink how we create and use our national parks and farms.

The water ribbon is another delicious plant used by Aboriginal people for food and fibre. Just like cumbungi it grows near water and helps with water filtration. These days, cattle eat lots of water ribbon and cumbungi because they are really nutritious.

What would happen if we returned to the old ways?

A wetland was brought back to a healthy state in Warrnambool in Victoria once some nearby factories closed down. Because of this, magpie geese returned to the swamps. These geese had almost been wiped out because of how we drained swamps and hunted them without proper regulations.

Thirty years ago, I worked with Ganai dancer and performer Jamie Thomas on a project to recover the magpie goose dance. Jamie had seen the return of the geese in that Warrnambool swamp and wanted to revive the cultural dance. He found an old drawing of dancers with the goose design and we painted the chests of local men so that the dance could come back to life. Watching his performance gave me many feelings. The return of the geese was mirrored by the return of the people's awareness of them. It's an example of environmental and cultural recovery.

Warrigal greens and cunjim winyu

Warrigal greens are also called Captain Cook's spinach. James Cook found it growing over Aboriginal houses and stole it to feed his sailors and cure them of scurvy (a sickness you get when you don't eat enough green vegetables).

This plant has high levels of vitamins and minerals and is salt tolerant, which means it will grow in places where many other green vegetables cannot.

When I was a kid, we were taught so little about Australia's history that I didn't even realise my old people grew vegetables like the warrigal greens. Some hills where I grew up were covered in the greens. We would get cardboard boxes and slide down the slopes. The greens made us go even faster!

Cunjim winyu is a tasty salad vegetable. It has a small yellow button flower in summer, but during autumn and spring it has a lovely fresh green top and looks wonderful on top of a salad or in an open sandwich.

We grow cunjim winyu plant on my farm. We served it to a top Australian chef, Ben Shewry, in 2021 and his eyes widened, and he couldn't stop talking about it. I think it beats the iceberg lettuce!

My home town is called Mallacoota. Have you ever been there? I was told that no Aboriginal people lived in Mallacoota. People have told me there were no massacres and therefore no forced removals of Aboriginal people off their land. But this isn't true.

Russell Mullet from the Ganai people found an old map of Mallacoota and passed it on to me. It was drawn by surveyor Francis MacCabe in 1847. The map showed the name of every river, hill, island and clearing in the local Aboriginal language. He must have got this information from Aboriginal people because MacCabe did not speak the language.

The map proved that Aboriginal people did live in Mallacoota.

Terra nullius is a term that describes a land owned by no one. To justify invasion, the Europeans said that no one owned Australia. They had to convince themselves and others that Aboriginal and Torres Strait Islander people were barely human. They had to prove that Aboriginal and Torres Strait Islander people did nothing with the land of Australia. But we know how wrong this idea was!

Grasses

We also found a coloured version of the map online and it showed us vegetation across open Country. It showed us where grasses grew. One area of Mallacoota today remains full of native grass because it's near an airport where no cattle or people are allowed.

My farm was allowed to harvest some grasses from the airport. We could then use that harvest to make flour and bake our own bread.

Tubers

Tubers are root vegetables.

Murnong is a tuber that can grow without extra water or fertiliser. Ash from cultural and controlled fires acts as fertiliser for the murnong.

Chefs love using it these days. The leaves can be eaten raw and when the root is cooked it looks like candied carrots. Doesn't that sound yum?

The white orchid was spread all over Melbourne and was a major food source for Aboriginal people. Now, though, the white orchid is almost extinct because of habitat destruction, sheep and the use of superphosphate.

Tubers can grow with grasses, and they can help improve soil. If we were to reintroduce these tubers and grasses on farms we wouldn't need to plough (dig) so much and other native root plants would be given the chance to grow and improve the lands.

Apples, cherries, currants and raspberries

Kangaroo apple trees (*Solanum laciniatum*) like disturbed or burnt ground and so they provide great protection for some soils. These trees have very sweet fruit that must be eaten ripe, but the birds know this too, so unprotected plants are raided early each day by honeyeaters, bowerbirds, wattlebirds and currawongs.

Aboriginal people picked the fruit before it was completely ripe and stored it in sand. Putting the apple in sand might have been to help it ripen or to help protect it from hungry animals.

I have always eaten the little cherries off cherry ballart trees (*Exocarpos cupressiformis*). The wood is good for boomerangs, and owls like to roost in the branches. The fruit is small and slightly musky but is high in vitamins B and C.

The native currant (*Coprosma quadrifida*) is a delicious fruit. It is tiny but full of flavour and vitamins. We have been harvesting it by tapping the trunk and branches so that the ripe fruit falls into a coolamon or onto a drop sheet.

The plant that I think has most potential to sell around Australia is the native raspberry (*Rubus parvifolius*). This was my Uncle Bill's favourite fruit, and he would get us to hunt for them in the gullies. It is not as juicy as the strawberries or raspberries that most Australians are used to, but it is highly nutritious and grows really well in Australian conditions.

At Yumburra we are raising kangaroo apple from seed. I am very excited about all the different ways Australia could use it! But with all this talk of growing native plants, we need to keep one important question in mind: how are Aboriginal people going to be included in its use and the profits from its sales?

Kurrajong

Chris Harris, an Aboriginal man and the farm manager at Yumburra, took us to explore Country up at Yambulla, an old property in the Australian Alps. The owner of this property wanted us to harvest his kangaroo and spear grasses and we got really good harvests.

Chris was also interested in the kurrajong (*Brachychiton populneus*) on the property, as he had learnt from his father and grandfather that his people used to eat the root of the tree. Yuin people used the slender rods of the kurrajong to make spears and fire drills. Aboriginal people created fire by twirling a hard narrow rod (often kurrajong wood) in a hole in a grass tree stem and they still do today. The fruit was also eaten after the sharp bristles were removed.

When we were up there, Chris dug up a small tree and we found that the root was sweet and filling. We are experimenting now with growing seedling kurrajong trees at Yumburra.

Sometimes these plants were deliberately planted to make a corridor and direct people to important sites on Country. We have tried to do this too and so our kurrajongs grow as a corridor to the heart of our farm. This is the sort of thing we try to do in order to honour our old people.

Grains and bread

Why are budgerigars disappearing? Early European 'explorers' and 'settlers' said that the centre of Australia was full of these birds. But today, the seeds on which the budgies fed have been destroyed by cattle, sheep, goats, donkeys, horses and buffalo. These hard-hoofed animals harden the soil and reduce its fertility and ability to hold water.

Do you know of the explorers Burke and Wills? When they were dying on Cooper Creek, the local Aboriginal people offered them nardoo flour made from seeds harvested from a plant that grew nearby. The local people soaked the seeds overnight to remove a toxin, but Burke and Wills ignored this knowledge and suffered because of it.

Aboriginal-baked products have been called dampers. (The word 'damper' is probably taken from an Aboriginal language: dangar is a word for bread products, and it is probable that Europeans pinched it.) Grinding stones found in Kakadu show that flour was made in Australia at least 65,000 years ago. This is long before any other society was known to make bread. So Aboriginal Australians were the world's first bakers!

For hundreds of years researchers didn't bother looking into Aboriginal and Torres Strait Islander histories in detail because they were more interested in places like Egypt, where they thought 'real' civilisation began. This hasn't been very helpful to our country.

Have you ever been to the Melbourne Museum? There is a team there that includes Aboriginal and non-Aboriginal curators and they have done a lot of research on Aboriginal bread and baking. When I saw this collection, I cried. It felt so important to me.

When making bread we usually need to add something to make the dough rise. Today we use baking powder or yeast that we buy from the shops.

But before invasion, Aboriginal people used different types of ingredients to make bread rise. I asked some young Aboriginal women working at the Art Gallery of New South Wales about it:

- One student was told about the method of soaking banksia flowers in water and allowing them to ferment.
- One had a grandfather who had been a camp cook and had added the whitest ash from a particular wood to bread.
- Another said her grandfather used to shoot galahs and use the partly fermented seed from the birds' crop as a rising agent (the bird holds the seed in a small pouch inside its neck so that it will ferment and become more easily digestible). And then he cooked the galah!

Aboriginal bee farming

Did you know that First Nations people in Australia had methods for farming native bees? Most people don't know this. In Europe there is a terrible disease that is impacting bees and bee farming. If Australia put in lots of effort to work with our native bees, we could make sure that we have honey and bees in the future.

The knowledge of caring for Country

I have shared some very important Aboriginal knowledge in this chapter and I am nervous about that. I'm nervous because Australians have a habit of stealing Aboriginal and Torres Strait Islander knowledge without giving credit or compensation to the original creators.

But I challenge you to make sure that you use this knowledge with care and that you let other people know who first farmed and cared for this land. We all have to make sure First Nations people are included in the Australian food world.

Your turn

Supporting local country, local business

- Consider the magpie goose story. When a wetland regenerated after factories were closed, the geese returned and the local Aboriginal people re-learnt their cultural dance. How would caring for Country help culturally and spiritually as well?
- Research how Australian First Nations businesses are making money and creating employment for their people through food and Country regeneration. You can start by searching for 'food' on the Supply Nation website directory for First Nations businesses: supplynation.org.au/.

Bushtucker gardens

- Look into establishing a bushtucker garden in your school, if you haven't already got one. If you have one, ask your teacher if you can use the produce in cooking and make sure it is being maintained and is accurately labelled. If you are establishing a new garden, talk with your local Aboriginal leaders, rangers or NRM (Natural Resource Management) representatives. Look up resources from the Junior Landcare Learning Centre (juniorlandcare.org.au) and Deadly Ed (deadlyed.com.au).

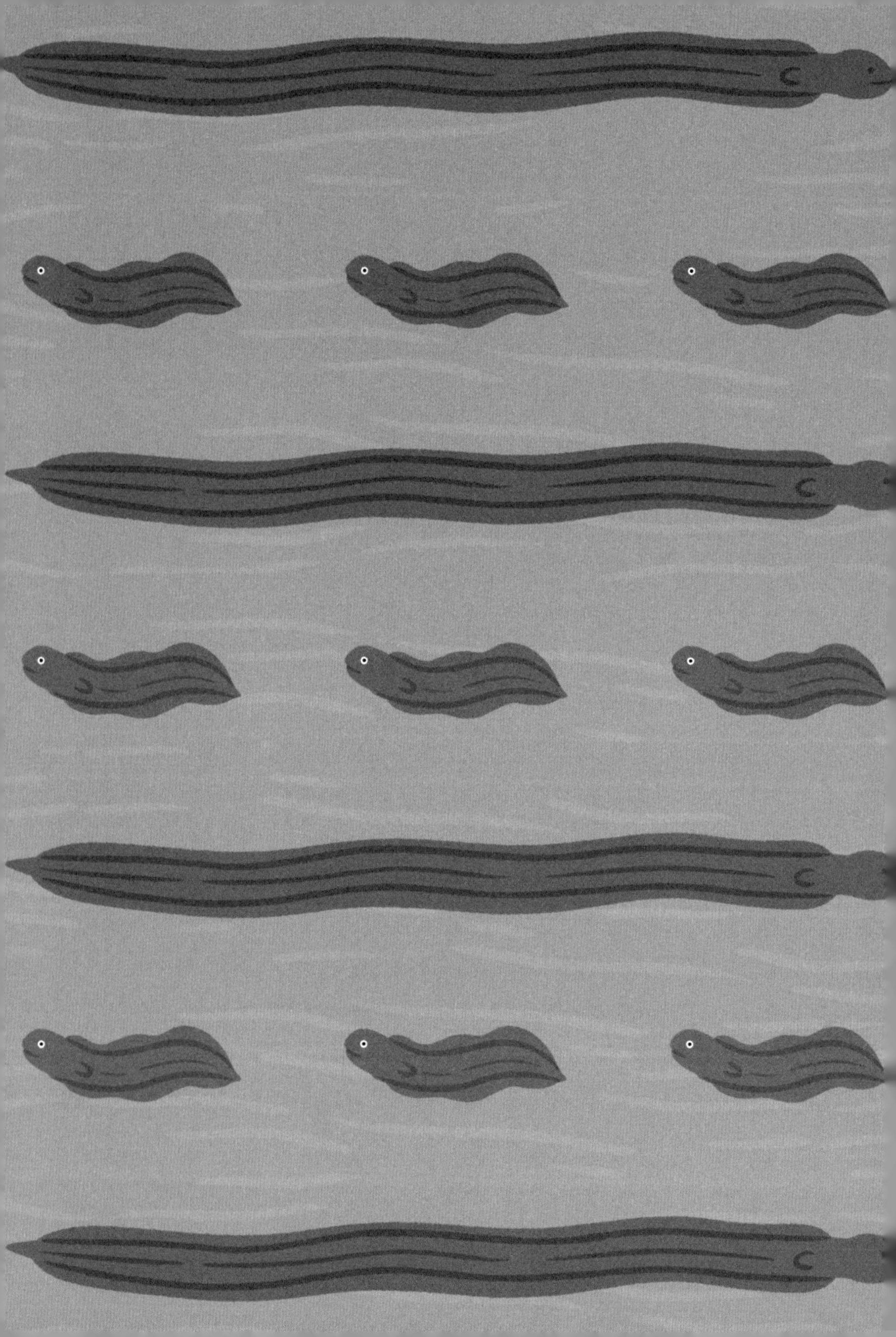

Chapter 7: by Bruce Pascoe

Future farming

Where do we get protein from?

Do you know what foods give you protein? Most people in Australia eat meat to get protein. But the meat most of us eat is not originally from Australia. These animals – hard-hoofed animals like cows – are not good for Australia's vegetation and soil. If you see flourishing farms these days, the farmers probably have to use harsh chemicals to help things grow.

When the Europeans invaded Australia, they wanted to turn the country into a little England. So, they imported animals that have now done a lot of damage to Australia. I wish they had chosen to love Australia for what it was.

Kangaroos and emus

In Australia, many farms allow kangaroos and emus to graze their lands. Kangaroos and emus are usually pest free, especially when they graze on land that doesn't have sheep or cattle. The meat of kangaroos and emus is lean and full of protein. It should be part of a clever diet in our country. But we've never farmed them. Why do you think this is?

I live out in the country, and I love to see relaxed animals like kangaroos around my home. Kangaroos around our farm find shade on a hot day and mothers will spoon up with their joeys. It is a very cute sight! But a calf (a baby cow) or a lamb (a baby sheep) is pretty cute too, and yet humans send them to be killed in awful conditions. I believe that if we eat meat, we should take responsibility for how that meat is prepared.

The cattle and sheep we eat today need to be drenched in chemical treatments. This is because we need to make sure they don't have footrot, lice, worms, bloat, scours, pinkeye, mastitis, flystrike, pneumonia and a hundred more health problems. Most of the chemicals used to treat them are so poisonous we can't eat the meat straight away. Kangaroos and emus don't need treatment like this when they graze on land without cattle.

To harvest kangaroos and emus before invasion, Aboriginal people used droving techniques, a type of hunting known as battue. They would lead the animals into a certain area steadily, so the animals didn't get spooked. They would guide them between wide wings made from timber and stone, to create an area like a very large funnel. These were so huge they could be around 40 kilometres apart at the beginning.

Aboriginal people also gathered young pelicans! Young, flightless birds were herded into yards and used for food. The old people used spears and net traps for emus and other birds.

Another form of protein

I have a suggestion for another form of gathering protein in Australia. It's roadkill. This might sound a bit off but this meat is edible and I hate waste. I have driven down roads in the mornings and seen the animals who have been hit by traffic: wallabies, kangaroos, possums and wombats. Sometimes I've seen kangaroos and wallabies with broken legs as the result of being hit by a car.

Once, I found a huge injured male kangaroo by following his moans of pain. I will never forget the look he gave me when I arrived with my gun. He knew exactly what was about to happen, and he was ready.

Why don't we use their bodies for food?

Animals killed by cars and trucks almost always die suddenly, which means their meat is tender. This is because their meat doesn't toughen like cattle meat because they don't sit in fear and release adrenaline (which toughens the muscles).

Why don't we have patrol vans with people licensed to inspect roadkill and harvest anything left that could be eaten by humans or even turned into dog food? We can check if the meat is okay by using a temperature probe.

Harvesting meat killed by our cars and farming kangaroo and emu stock would mean we could have fewer hard-hoofed animals like cows, which are harmful to our lands.

Seafood

Fishing methods today are not very sustainable – they won't last into the future. For example, seagrasses are vital for the survival of hundreds of creatures and yet when humans fish for scallops, the seagrass is destroyed by the machines. This kills millions of worms and crustacea.

Apollo Bay, in Victoria, used to be home to massive schools of barracouta. The schools were caught and transported on trucks to the fish market in Footscray. Often, by the time the fish arrived, as much as 100 per cent of the catch had started to spoil. But that did not stop the fishers. 'See fish, must have fish' is their motto and they wasted so much fish it was very sad.

Crayfish, or southern rock lobster, are now in danger of extinction because of humans. My father used to buy a crayfish every Friday night for a dollar but today they are $120 a kilo! Chinese and Japanese demand has pushed the price of crayfish up, making them very expensive for Australians. But the biggest danger to crayfish is overfishing.

I used to catch crayfish for my old Uncle Banjo Clarke, and he was always quick to inspect it to see what sex it was. The day I gave him a female, he lectured me very gently about sustainability. Catching female crayfish makes it hard for the crayfish to keep their numbers up. Uncle Banjo Clarke was a beautiful man but a stern protector of the environment. Never kill females unless you want populations to decrease!

Bycatch is a word that means accidentally catching fish or seabirds when they aren't the target. Sometimes other fish and animals will be caught in a fishing net even though the humans fishing don't want them. Bycatch is harming the numbers of fish in our seas. Some nets have been improved so that bycatch doesn't happen as much, but it is still unsustainable.

In New South Wales, 30 per cent of reef fish in the past ten years were lost. If this happens again over the next ten years, our fish stocks may never recover. We must demand that we don't kill unwanted fish in the pursuit of other animals.

Did you know that overpopulation and excessive food consumption (eating too much) also hurts our oceans? This is because the demand for seafood grows so high that it urges people to overfish and fish dangerously. There aren't enough fish left in the sea. We need to take fewer fish so that fish populations are maintained, otherwise there won't be any fish at all.

What do we do now?

The current methods of fishing need to be stopped. Here is a list of some things I think we can do:

- Be careful of how big our population gets and how much we eat (and throw away).
- Make prices of seafood more expensive so we don't consume too much. This will help the fisher people who rely on it for an income. They catch fewer fish but still make enough money to survive. But then we also need to make sure every family has sufficient money to buy food.
- Reduce the amount of seafood we collect.
- Look at different methods to gain protein (kangaroo and emus).
- Learn about how Aboriginal and Torres Strait Islander peoples farmed animals and fished seafoods before invasion.
- We need to pay the real price of animals and seafood.
- The cost to the environment must be included in the price of the animal. We need to think about how we can make sure our land and sea animals survive for the future. Can you imagine your great-grandchildren or your family in one hundred years? Let's promise to leave them with a beautiful world, not one emptied by our waste and greed.

Your turn

A healthy family diet

- Have you tried kangaroo? Look up the prices for kangaroo and beef steaks, stirfry and mince. Compare packs with the same weight and see what price they are. Are there major differences in the prices of beef and kangaroo?
- Find out the differences in carbon emissions and greenhouse gases that are released by farming cattle, sheep and kangaroos (see Agrifutures article 'Kangaroos could be the key to increasing red meat supply and reducing emissions', agrifutures.com.au/ews/kangaroos-could-be-the-key-to-increasing-red-meat-supply-and-reducing-emissions/). Do you think that beef should be more expensive than kangaroo?

First Nations fishing

- Learn more about First Nations fishing practices. Some resources to help are listed below. Brewarrinna Fish Traps: 'Baiames Ngunnhu – the story of Brewarrina Fish Traps' by Department of the Environment and Heritage with Aunty June Barker, and a series by New South Wales fisheries called 'How to catch sea tucker': series of eight videos by New South Wales fisheries, both of which can be found on YouTube.

Chapter 8:
by Bill Gammage

Our country needs help

Open forest in 1788

Let's remind ourselves of what land in Australia was like before invasion. There was lots of variety. Early Europeans saw that the land was different to England. In many places they could drive a horse and cart through land which is thick forest today. The land didn't have too much scrub either, which meant that this deadly layer of fire fuel was less common and more confined. Much grassland from 1788 is forest and scrub now.

Francis MacCabe was a surveyor in 1847. His map from back then tells us he saw 'open forest', some of which is thick forest today. MacCabe also mapped alternating patches of thick and open forest, woodland and grass. Aboriginal people made this mosaic of land with fire and no fire.

Big fires

It's tragic that big, dangerous fires have become 'normal' in Australia. We expect them now. This started not long after Europeans invaded. One example is a fire in Victoria in 1851. Bullock drivers left burning logs alone in the Plenty Ranges, and the winds took over and snagged the flames. A massive fire started. It was so terrible that birds died in flight. Twelve people and over a million sheep died. Thousands of other animals were lost too. Around five million hectares were burnt – that's around 22 per cent of Victoria!

But the newcomers didn't learn from their mistakes. Fires kept starting and kept killing.

Checklist when predicting big fires:

- A drought summer – when the country hasn't received enough rain in the hot months.
- Allowing remote fires to burn – fires in hard-to-reach places being left to burn without any management or firefighting.
- A very hot peak day – when the temperature reaches sweltering levels above 40 degrees Celsius.
- Hot northerlies – when strong winds blow from the north.

Do you know what to look out for?

A town called Mallacoota

Mallacoota is a town in Gippsland, Victoria. It's where Francis MacCabe drew his 1847 map I told you about. Maybe you've been there. My friend Bruce Pascoe lives near there.

Before invasion, Aboriginal people cared for this area. They made sure fuel didn't build up because they knew the land had potential to create a giant bushfire. But after invasion, fuel began to increase, and the danger of a bushfire grew.

In 1919, Victoria made a rule that 'no fire' was best to take care of land. This meant very few controlled burns, and no cultural burnings were allowed. This let fuel build up over the years.

The people who lived in Mallacoota knew the danger of this policy. Some said they'd go to the beach if a big fire came. Others agreed that there may be a fire but didn't think it would be too dangerous.

In 2019, Black Summer happened. It began with hot winds, drought and lots of fuel. An unstoppable firestorm raged through Mallacoota. People had to flee to the beach because the town was so unsafe, and even then they had to be rescued by boats. White ash covered the area and white ash usually means that fires have risen over 1000 degrees Celsius.

RESCUE
RESCUE

After Black Summer

Something important to remember is that although Mallacoota and areas nearby experienced terrible fires in 2019–20, the centre and north of Australia didn't. Fires that happen in the centre and the north of Australia are mostly always controlled. Why do you think this is?

In the south of Australia, we focus on saving lives once a fire has started. In the north and in the centre, people focus on preventing fires and controlling them.

We have the best tools to fight fires in most of Australia, but I don't think we are very organised about stopping them before they start.

Firefighting is a dangerous and brave job. At the moment, firefighters are controlled by each state's government. One day they may even be controlled by the national government. But I don't think this is a good thing. Fires change depending on where they are. We need local knowledge to help us control and contain them. When the people in charge of fire-fighting don't live in the area where there is a fire, it can make things move slowly. It means local firefighters have to wait for instructions from people outside their district.

The key is learning to prevent fire. We need to learn how to reduce fuel throughout the year. We need to learn to work with fire and see it as a friend and not as an enemy.

Black Summer facts:

In just six months three billion living creatures were killed or displaced by the Black Summer fires.

Europeans created, and still create, dangerous wilderness by neglecting to care for the land in the way Aboriginal people had done for thousands of years.

Many people who are descended from the invading Europeans don't understand the land and don't trust the methods of care that First Nations people use. How does that make you feel? Do you think you've learnt something that can help you care for Country and make a positive change to our home?

Important ways fire was used before invasion:

1. It gave plants and animals the fire they needed to thrive.
2. It maintained a diversity of plants by spreading seeds and refreshing plants.
3. It gave every creature a welcoming habitat.
4. It ensured an abundance of everything.
5. It helped make resources like food and shelter easy to find and predictable.
6. It prevented big killer fires like those of Black Summer.

What to do now?

What would your suggestion be if you were put in charge of fire control?

Lots of us think that being Australian means being able to look after our houses, our backyards, and the things we individually own. But many Australians really want to care for the whole country, even places where they don't live! To achieve caring for all of Australia, we have a long way to go. Here are some suggestions on what we, as Australians, could do next:

One

We need to think about fire throughout the whole year, not just during the summer months. Fuel gathers during the whole year. We should use the first months of winter to cool-burn patches to break up scrub and regrow some plants. These clearings can then become safe places for animals and people, even as the bush grows up around them.

Two

We should think about fire use in two categories: fire and no fire. If we learn more about this Aboriginal way of fire farming we could have a much safer environment. We need to listen to people on Country and to people with the knowledge of using fire.

Three

Let's learn to burn and burn to learn, guided by Aboriginal experts and by firefighters with fire experience. As we do that, we will learn more. We will learn to prevent fires.

Four

Decisions and resources should be local. If they are made by people who don't live near the fire or understand fire, things won't work out. We need to create local fire prevention programs that train people from a young age.

Five

Cultural burning is an important part of fire. First Nations cultural knowledge that connects to fire should be respected and valued. How do you think we can make sure this knowledge is helped to grow?

Six

Ask Aboriginal experts to take the lead in showing the rest of Australia how frequent fires can protect native species. Non-Indigenous people can't just steal this knowledge and hope for the best. We need to listen to those who have the knowledge. I can imagine senior First Nations Elders working in environmental policy positions. I can also imagine a ranger program that spans the country. Imagine if rural fire brigades and Aboriginal experts worked together!

Imagine if there were no more Black Summers. Imagine if fire was a friend to all the people, plants and animals in Australia.

First Nations people never needed all the tools of European farming. Fire was their tool, and their ally. Together fire and people managed the whole of Australia. There was no wilderness in 1788. People didn't waste resources; instead they worked hard to make sure their Country was productive and beautiful for their children, for the generations to come, and for all creation. They made sure the continent was balanced, and left the world as they found it. They thought of future generations. Shouldn't we also?

Your turn

Taking action for our future

- Discuss the six suggestions for how we could change our future by changing our fire and land care practices. Create a draft digital poster or infographic to demonstrate the key points.
- Interview local Aboriginal rangers or NRM employees and local firefighting authorities, including Rural Fire Service volunteers. Ask them about their opinions on the key points above. Ask them what students, families and community members can do to help (volunteering, land care projects, etc.).

Reflecting on the past

- Considering what we have been learning in this book, do you think the word 'invaded' is the right word to describe European arrival to this land? Why or why not?
- Families who have a long tradition of European farming on this land might be worried that moving to Aboriginal practices would be too difficult and expensive, or reduce their profits. What solutions can you think of that would respect all people's heritage and connections to this land?

Chapter 9:
by Bruce Pascoe

How we might love Mother Earth more

What do you love most about our world? Do you have a favourite animal? Or a favourite plant? Is there a spot that you and your friends or family visit all the time? I believe that there are so many things in our world to love and we have a responsibility to protect them.

It's not smart to use up all the good resources on Earth. Shouldn't we make sure there are beautiful animals, plants and holiday spots for the future?

Forestry and mining

Did you know that when humans build houses, they use lots and lots of timber? Much of this timber is wasted as it is sent to landfill or burnt. Why do we let this happen? I bet if we made timber more expensive then builders would not want to waste it as much.

There is a tree in East Gippsland that I want to talk about. It is called the silvertop ash (*Eucalyptus sieberi*). It's a tree that grows straight. Its first branches are high off the ground, and it is perfect for harvesting. Most of these trees are sent to be turned into woodchips. Woodchips, which Australia sells for a very cheap price, are very unsustainable. But companies that chop down these trees are given lots of money and are helped by the government.

Should we rethink this method? Maybe timber and woodchips shouldn't be so cheap? Maybe they shouldn't be used as often as they are?

When I say we should cut down trees a little less, some people tell me that that would mean too many Australians would lose their jobs. But less people work in forestry than we think. In the 1970s, we would see teams of fifteen people working in the forest. In 2021, I saw two major forestry operations where only one person was working with one truck, one harvester and one loader.

The Australian Government taxes tobacco and alcohol because they are dangerous. If they tax these items, it makes us less likely to buy them. Shouldn't we also use this method to change the way we use our trees?

An artist called Craig Ruddy and his partner Roberto Meza Mont organised a fundraising event to raise money for Black Duck Foods, an Aboriginal social enterprise out of Yumburra farm. The money would help Black Duck Foods employ local Yuin people to produce traditional Aboriginal foods at my farm in Yumburra.

They ran raffles and auctioned one of Craig's paintings. There was so much support! Everyone wanted to see more sustainable agricultural practices.

A portion of this money is being used to support students in local schools, some of whom already work a few days at our farm. For those who enjoy it we will try to help them plan a way into agricultural science or any other course that could support them in working on a farm.

Some of the other money will help us design and manufacture a new seed harvester. We will call this machine Mandu II (Bandicoot II).

Dunnarts and bandicoots

Cats and foxes are very cute animals. Unfortunately, they are also one of the biggest threats to Australia's native wildlife. If we can control them, we could see the widespread return of bandicoots and dunnarts.

I'd never seen a dunnart until I was moving a bunch of burnt logs after some fires. A group of the little creatures hopped out like mini kangaroos (closely followed by a tiger snake). These beautiful animals are seed eaters and they came back to the land because the grass came back. The grass came back because we removed cattle from our farm, which allowed the grass to seed and grow.

Bandicoots have a big job in this ecosystem. They eat small fungi in the soil. When they dig for the fungi they make small holes in the ground which are little beds for raindrops and seeds. This helps everything grow beautifully. Bandicoots churn tonnes of soil each year – creating wonderful mulch.

A different way of seeing the world

Did you know that in wealthy countries such as Australia, Britain and the United States there are very high rates of sad and lonely adults? It seems to me that lots of people like to escape from their lives. But why?

The world has received some enormous benefits from science and engineering, but not everything invented by people has been good for the world. Bombs and harmful gases are just some examples. Chains that couldn't be broken were made by intelligent engineers, but they were used to keep Aboriginal people captive in Australia. After World War II, Australia allowed the British to test nuclear weapons in Maralinga in South Australia. It was considered a desert, but Maralinga was home to the Tjarutja people. There was hardly any effort made by the government to let them know about the nuclear testing. It took around twenty years for the rest of Australia to find out about it.

People say: you can't make an omelette without breaking eggs. But I don't believe that's the right way to think about life.

I believe we shouldn't create things or live in a way that's harmful just because we can or just because it's easier.

How could our future look?

In other Western nations, the people in charge have decided that some agricultural chemicals are too dangerous for the land and animals, so they banned them. Australia is still using many of those chemicals, but we could do more to control them.

Blaming drought

Farmers often struggle in Australia and Australians like to blame it on drought. Drought has also been blamed for:

- fish kills in the Murray-Darling;
- clouds of dust in the air every summer;
- wildfires that destroy homes.

But it's not drought that's the problem. It's our management (or mismanagement) of the land. We need to do better.

After the 2019–20 fires, we had to rebuild sheds and add new ones, and we used many poles from the forest. We are planning to harvest all the small trees on our property and sell them to a milling contractor. Thinning our forest will provide us with income and help us reach our goal of having ten to twelve big trees to the acre, the pre-1788 principle of Aboriginal Australia. The aim is for the forest in our district to include a variety of types: grey box, red ironbark, stringybark, silvertop ash and a balance of smaller shrubs.

Of course, this forest plan must be maintained for at least fifty years, but we are doing it for the sake of our grandchildren and great-grandchildren.

What can we do?

I think we should form a treaty between Aboriginal and Torres Strait Islander peoples and non-Indigenous Australians. A treaty might look different in different parts of Australia. It would be agreements made between the local Aboriginal or Torres Strait Islander peoples and governments. It could give power back to First Nations Australians to work and care for their Country. I believe young people are our future, so it's important to work with them. We should also be able to talk about Country and listen with respect to each other's ideas.

What do you think Australians can do to care for our land? Is there anything you will do now that you've read this book? The time has come for us to make changes. We need to grow into a people with great love for our country.

Your turn

Exploring sustainable housing

- Explore the 'Your home' website to find out more about the waste issues created by building, the other materials available, and the ways to reduce waste and build more sustainable homes. Write a summary of at least five ideas you find interesting on the website and share with a family member or friend.

Regenerating threatened species

- We learnt about the bandicoot and dunnart, and how cats and foxes threaten them. If we could manage foxes and cats, these creatures could regenerate. Find out about other endangered Australian species, their role in the ecosystem, why they are endangered, and what can be done to help them.

Forest plan

- Uncle Bruce has a forest plan for his farm to return to pre-1788 numbers of trees and balance of species. Research how species such as grey box, red ironbark, stringybark, silvertop ash contribute to our native habitats and ecosystem. Do any of these grow in your local area? Do you have important trees that you would include in a forest plan for your area?

About the creators

Bruce Pascoe

is a Bunurong, Yuin and Tasmanian Aboriginal writer of literary fiction, non-fiction, poetry, essays and children's literature. He is the enterprise professor in Indigenous Agriculture at the University of Melbourne. He is best known for his work *Dark Emu: Aboriginal Australia and the Birth of Agriculture* (Magabala Books 2014).

Bill Gammage

is a historian at the Humanities Research Centre, Australian National University. His books include *The Broken Years: Australian Soldiers in the Great War* and three prize-winning titles – *Narrandera Shire, The Sky Travellers: Journeys in New Guinea 1938-1939* and *The Biggest Estate on Earth: How Aborigines Made Australia.*

Savi Ross

is an African American, Torres Strait Islander illustrator based in Narrm Melbourne. Savi's illustrations often feature playful colour, friendship, and, most importantly, people of colour loving themselves and each other. Savi's illustrations are expressed through prints, zines and more, where they think about community and the joys of place and family. None of their work would be possible without real mountains, real love, and the many Black creatives who occupy space and beyond digital art.

Jasmin McGaughey

is a Torres Strait Islander and African American writer and editor. She is the author of the Little Ash series and her debut young adult novel is *Moonlight and Dust*.

Important words and concepts

cool fire: a fire lit on purpose where there is little fuel and damp or cool conditions. The flames are always low, and don't ignite shrubs or trees. They are lit to help protect camps and special places and reduce fuel, and refresh plants that need fire to flourish.

Dreaming: an understanding of the world and its creation. Creator Ancestors made Country in the Dreaming, and they still watch over it. The Dreaming requires each generation of people leaves the world as they found it.

firestick farming: a land management technique where vegetation is burnt to reduce fuel for large fires and encourage new growth. Animals, such as kangaroos, then come to eat the fresh grass.

fuel load: scrub, leaves and trees that ignite and can cause an inferno. A light fuel load means there is not much fuel for a fire and a heavy fuel load means there is a lot of fuel for a fire.

hot fire: a fire with high flames. Hot fires were used rarely, but they could help clean up Country that is dirty or overrun with weeds, or help clear trees and stop scrub germinating.

intellectual property: ideas and information that belong to the person or people who created it. There are legal systems for protecting these ideas and making sure people are compensated for them.

land degradation: when land becomes less healthy and productive, usually because of humans' actions.

salination: when fresh water sources are overtaken by salt water and are no longer able to sustain plant and animal life as before.

scar trees: trees where sections of bark have been removed to make a canoe or coolamon.

Songlines: an ancient knowledge system that links together places, people and Country critical for survival. They are continuous and constantly updated.

Terra nullius: a term that describes a land owned by no one. Europeans said that no one owned Australia to justify the invasion.

topsoil: the top layer of soil where plants do most of their growing.

understorey: the lower level of growth in forests. In Australia it is often scrub that builds up under bigger plants and provides fuel to lift flames up high.

Index

About the series

The First Knowledges for younger readers series is based on the award-winning adult books. Other books in the series are:

Songlines by Margo Neale and Lynne Kelly

Design & Building on Country by Alison Page and Paul Memmott

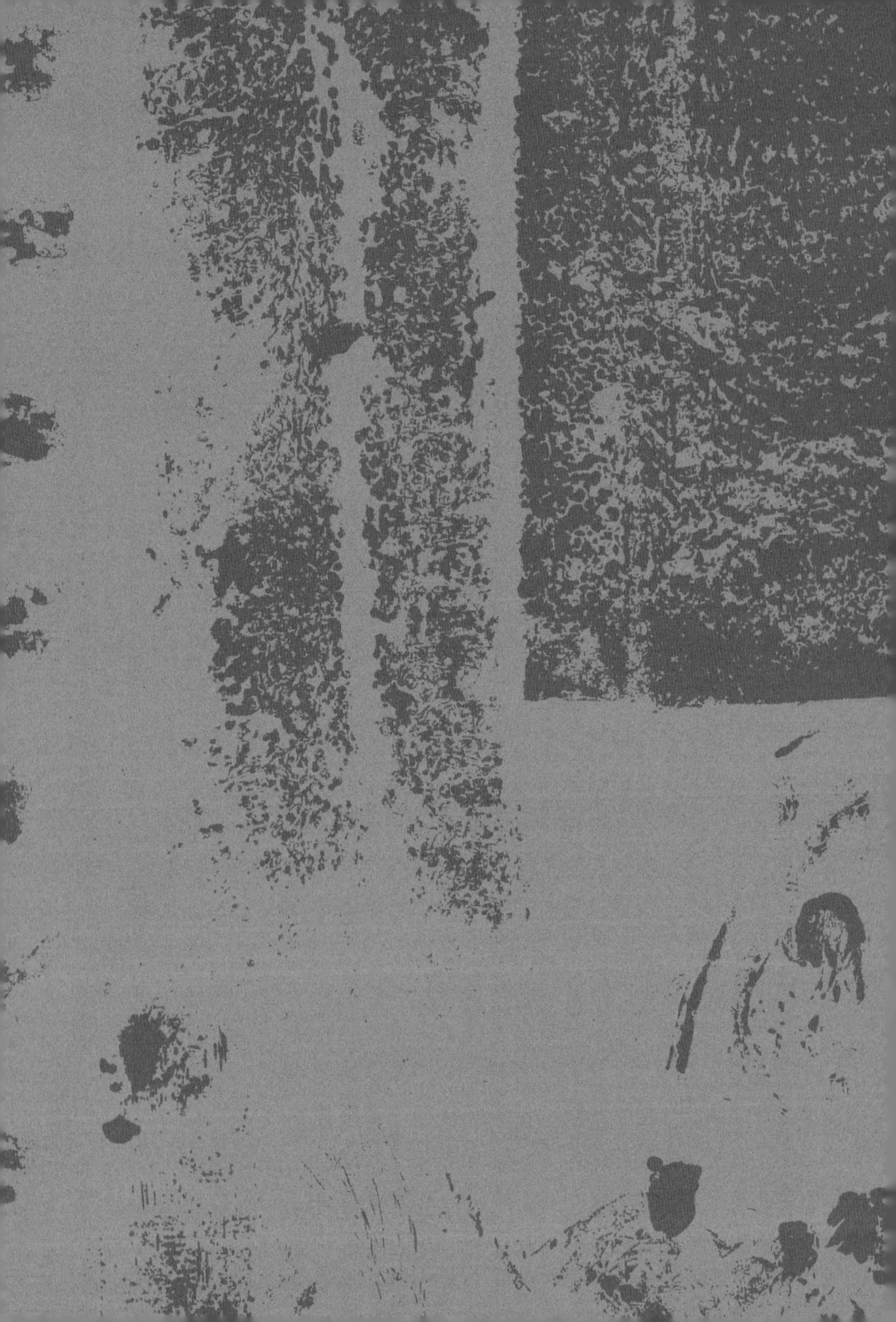